AF885082

The Master Key Credit BLUEPRINT VOL.2

For more resources, please visit https://www.ofpsagency.com

The Master Key Credit BLUEPRINT VOL.2

Stacey M. Oliver

Olivers Financial Planning Services, LLC ®™

South Carolina

For more resources, please visit https://www.ofpsagency.com

Disclaimer

The advice contained in this guide may not be suitable for everyone. The author obtained information from sources that may be reliable and from her own experience. The information in this guide is provided for education and informational purposes only, without any express or implied warranty of any kind, including warranties of accuracy, completeness for any particular purpose. The material contained in this guide is not intended to be and does not constitute financial, legal or any other advice. The information is general in nature and is not specific to you the user or anyone else. The author, distributor and publisher particularly disclaims any liability, loss or risk taken by individuals who directly or indirectly act on the information contained herein. All readers must accept all and full responsibilities for their use of this material. All pictures used in this guide are for illustrated purposes only. The pictures are only licensed for use of this guide and must not be used for any other purpose without prior written permission of the rights holder.

Copyrights

Work Cited
(https://en.oxforddictionaries.com/, n.d.)
(https://en.wikipedia.org/wiki/, n.d.)
(https://www.merriam-webster.com/, since 1828)
(https://www.investopedia.com/ask/answers/040715/how-does-your-checking-account-affect-your-credit-score.asp)
(https://www.creditkarma.com/article/CreditCardUtilizationAndScore)
(https://www.discover.com/free-credit-score)
(https://www.annualcreditreport.com/yourRights.action, since 2017)

Printed and Published in the United States of America

The Master Key Credit BLUEPRINT VOL.2
STACEY M. OLIVER

ISBN-13: 978-1-7350929-2-8

Interior Designs by STACEY M. OLIVER

A New Kind of Agency

Olivers Financial Planning Services, LLC

(aka OFPS, LLC) was incorporated and founded by Stacey M. Oliver, CEO, in 2015. Our mission is to create, enlighten, and empower committed effective stewards of finances. Our primary objective is to increase our clients' financial literacy awareness so they can fully understand how money works.

"Money can work hard for you instead of you working hard for it. Once that concept is learned then the vicious cycle and hold of debt can be removed."

OFPS

For more resources, please visit https://www.ofpsagency.com

For more resources, please visit https://www.ofpsagency.com

Hello

Hi, I'm ***Stacey M. Oliver***, your Financial Locksmith.

I empower individuals with the <u>Master Key</u> to unlocking doors to financial freedom.

Now let me ask...What is keeping the doors locked to you obtaining total financial freedom? The answer is simple, *Barrier(s).* A barrier is an obstacle that prevents movement, access, or progress.

If you do not become empowered with the Master Key to complete financial freedom the trend of financial barriers and financial ignorance will continue to filter and recycle through you and/or your family.

If the financial barrier is not broken and destroyed in our lives there will not be a financial legacy left for our next generation. Stop allowing the doors to remain locked to your financial freedom. **Possess the Master Key and start taking charge of unlocking doors to your financial wealth so you can begin to experience Financial FREEDOM.**

The Master Key Credit Blueprint workbook will increase your credit awareness. Constantly enhancing your credit is a lifestyle and a persisted process. Use this volume to improve and transition from common credit to first-rate credit.

The Credit Blueprint is indispensable to grasp the key elements of your credit score, familiarizing yourself with the three recommendations to retaining low revolving credit utilization and how to properly use credit cards for your advantage. Thank you for adding this workbook to your repertoire to successfully sustain and position your credit score rating in the sweet spot (750 – UP).

Table of Contents

CREDIT

"Knowledge, The Master Key to Financial Freedom."

-Stacey M. Oliver

Credit

Strong credit opens various gateways for the duration of regular day to day existence. You need your future to be better than your past…CHANGE. Why not choose the decision to change your present credit standing? Be certain your credit reflects positive change.

Constantly improving your credit is a lifestyle and a continued process. You may agree that it is very easy to fall in one of these categories:

Bad Credit
- Mismanaging Money
- Forfeiting/Neglecting Obligations

No Credit
- No Existing Credit Established
- Non-Sufficient Amount of Credit History

Over Extended Credit
- Too Many Credit Obligations
- Amount of Credit too Large to Pay

How to Build Credit

The High Fives to Building Credit

- Secure credit cards is one way to establish credit.
- Become an authorized user for an existing responsible cardholder. Ensure activity is being reported to ALL three credit agencies.
- Utilize a major credit card for normal regular expenditures, such as; gas, utilities, groceries, etc. and payoff current balance.
- Do NOT become greater than 30 days delinquent on any credit reporting accounts.
- Take advantage of a Credit Builder Program.

Credit FICO Score Model

FICO Score is a registered trademark of the Fair Isaac Corporation in United States and other countries.

Note: TransUnion uses the FICO score model.

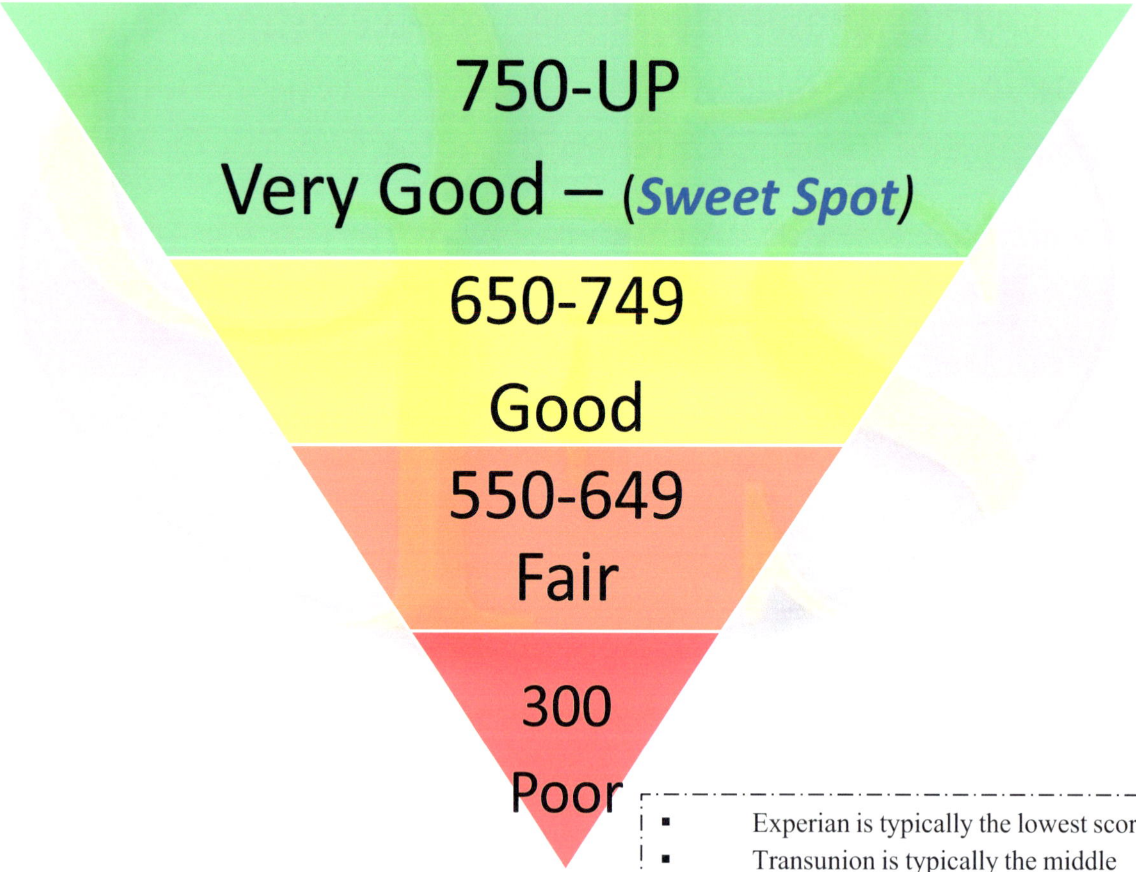

- Experian is typically the lowest score
- Transunion is typically the middle score
- Equifax is typically the highest score

FICO Credit Score

Key Pointers

- Establishing a good credit mixture such as installment loans and revolving credit influences 10% of your FICO Score. *(For example; car loan, credit card/line of credit, student loan, mortgage, etc.)*
- Length of Credit, also known as Aged Accounts, impacts 15% of FICO Score. *(Note: When disputing items reflecting negatively on credit report, the dispute may cause the clock to start over for the length of time the items will remain on report. For example; if a collection item is due to fall off the credit report within six months and a dispute is filed within the six months, the item will not fall off as scheduled but it will remain another 7 years from the date of the dispute.)*
- Inquiries make up 10% of your FICO Score.
- Revolving Utilization effects 30% of your FICO Score. *(Note: Simply keep all credit card balances below the 30% ratio or less of the credit card limit to ensure the utilization ratio is being maintained.)*
- On-time payments impact 35% of your FICO score.

Credit Score Impact

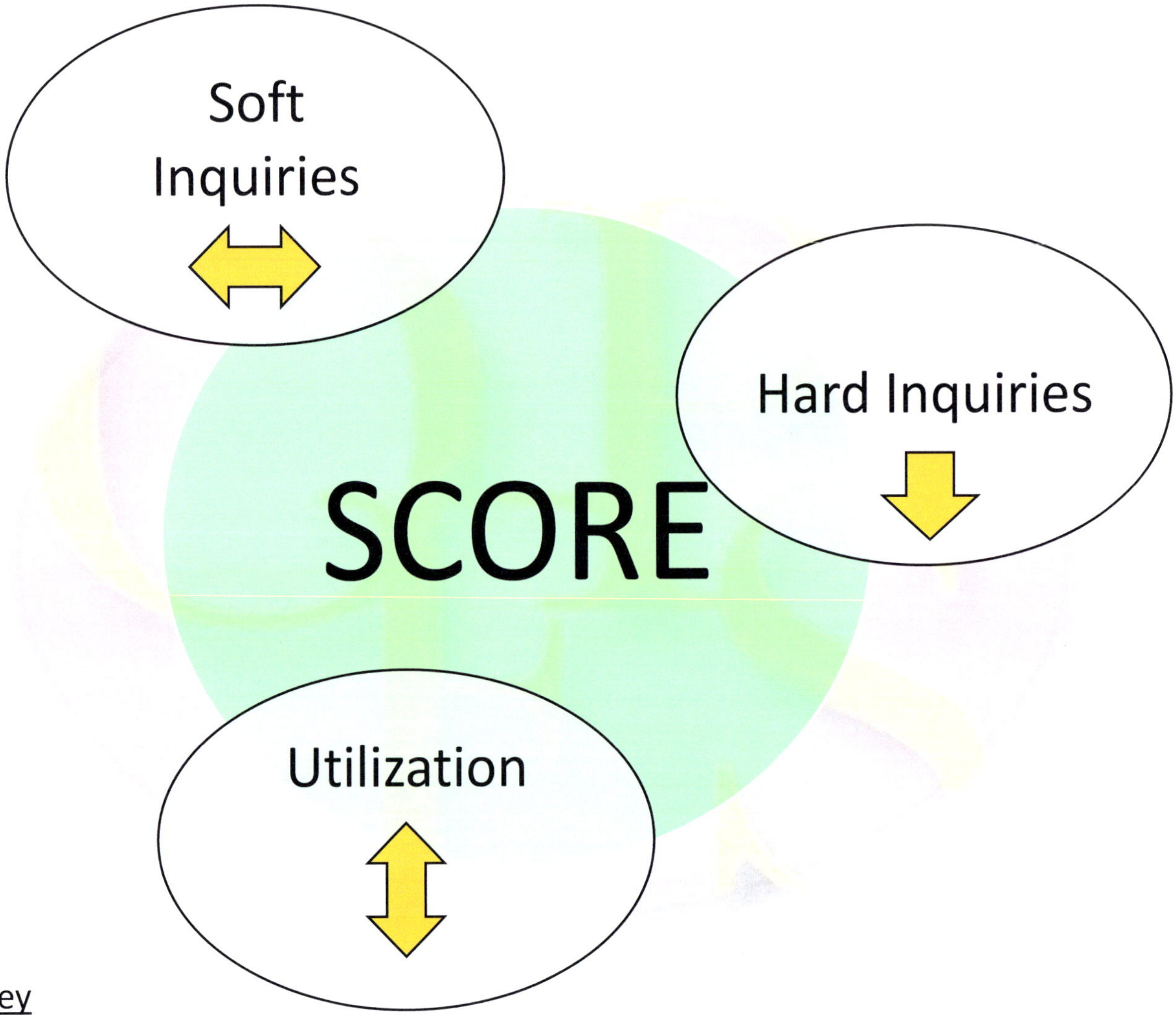

Key

Up or Down

No Impact

Down

Credit Score Impact *continued…*

I. Soft Inquiries: is when an individual credit is pulled when seeking employment, when an individual checks their own credit or pre-approvals for an offer. These inquiries do not impact your credit at all.

II. Hard Inquiries: is when an individual's credit is pulled when seeking to apply for credit accounts or loans. These inquiries can be a good indicator forasmuch credit seeking activity is kept at a minimum. Too many hard inquiries can negatively impact score.

III. Utilization: is an indicator of how much is owed on revolving credit accounts. This is one of the most important factors that impacts the credit score. A high ratio can reflect poorly on a person's credit score. The ratio will go up and down with payments and purchases. A good rule of thumb is to keep the ratio between 20 to 30 percent. Of course, lower the ratio the better.

Note: Mortgage payments usually have a major impact on credit score. Missing a payment could cause a tremendous drop in score.

Credit Utilization

Three Tips to Keep Utilization Low

- ✓ Making multiple revolving credit payments during one month. *(Note: Multiple payments may not avoid the next payment due for the following month. In other words, extra payments are not meant to be as paying it forward or used for a skip payment option. The next bill statement will be issued for the following month for payment amount due.)*
- ✓ Using revolving credit and spreading charges across multiple cards each month will avoid charging to or over the credit limit.
- ✓ Increase available credit if maintaining excellent credit and income has increased or little debt has been maintained.

Configure your utilization (divide the outstanding balance by the credit line and convert to percent) by completing the worksheet on the next page.

Extra worksheets have been provided.

Credit Utilization

NAME OF REVOLVING ACCOUNT	TOTAL BALANCE OWED	TOTAL CREDIT LINE	CONFIGURE UTILIZATON % (Balance/Credit Line)

A rule of thumb…keep the revolving utilization below 25%.

For more resources, please visit https://www.ofpsagency.com

Credit Utilization

NAME OF REVOLVING ACCOUNT	TOTAL BALANCE OWED	TOTAL CREDIT LINE	CONFIGURE UTILIZATON % (Balance/Credit Line)

A rule of thumb…keep the revolving utilization below 25%.

Credit Utilization

NAME OF REVOLVING ACCOUNT	TOTAL BALANCE OWED	TOTAL CREDIT LINE	CONFIGURE UTILIZATON % (Balance/Credit Line)

A rule of thumb…keep the revolving utilization below 25%.

For more resources, please visit https://www.ofpsagency.com

Test Your Knowledge

Utilization: is an indicator of how much is owed on revolving credit accounts. This is one of the most important factors that impacts the credit score. Which of the following is a TRUE statement?

- ❑ A high ratio can reflect poorly on a person's credit score.
- ❑ The ratio will go up and down with payments and purchases.
- ❑ All of the above.

❑ All of the above. Correct Answer

OFPS

Credit Tips

Six Tips to Improve Credit Score

- ✓ Check your credit reports at least every 12 months.
- ✓ Pay your bills on-time. *(Remember, when making an extra mortgage payment do not include with regular payment. Instead, issue a separate payment and apply ONLY to principal.)*
- ✓ Evaluate/lower your credit utilization to ensure it is below at least 30%.
- ✓ Do not close or delete old accounts reflecting positively on credit report.
- ✓ Don't apply for too much new credit. *(This will affect Debt to Income (DTI) ratio. Keep DTI ratio at least at 35% which includes recurring debt, mortgage, auto, credit cards, etc. A low Debt to Income ratio indicates sufficient income relative to debt and it is more attractive to lenders/creditors.)*
- ✓ Identify and change unhealthy credit behavior.

Credit Cards

DO'S and DON'TS

- DO NOT max out your credit cards.
- DO NOT charge over your credit limit. (*Caution; some credit card companies will allow you to go over your credit line.*)
- Avoid making the monthly minimum required payment.
- Request lower interest rate on your credit cards. Just because you were approved at an interest rate when you applied for card you do not have to remain at the initial rate.
- Keep your outstanding balances on your credit cards 20% - 30% of the credit limit. The lower the better.
- DO NOT pay all your credit cards to a zero balance.
- Stay away from too many department stores credit cards. They tend to carry high interest rates.
- It is a good idea to have 2 major credit cards and one department store credit card.
- Avoid credit cards with annual fees.
- Make credit cards work in your favor. Apply for cards that provide rewards and/or points to use toward airfare, hotels, products, gift cards etc.
- DO NOT use credit cards for cash you do not have.
- Pay regular monthly bills with major credit card if possible. In return use the cash payments that were going to be used to pay bills towards paying off credit card.

EQUIFAX, EXPERIAN, & TRANSUNION

All credit report companies contain basically the same information but may be in a different format.

- Knowing what's in your credit file is very important. Why? To avoid or correct any existing errors, mistakes and/or inaccuracies that can have a negative impact on your score.

- Request to get a copy of your Consumer Credit Report from all three nationwide credit reporting agencies. (*Note: A copy can be requested once every 12 months from each agency.*) Once received, review and verify all information is correct.

For more information on obtaining your free credit report visit www.annualcreditreport.com or call 1-877-322-8228. Deaf and hard of hearing consumers can access the TDD service by calling 7-1-1 and referring the Relay Operator to 1-800-821-7232.

Take Action

Test Your Knowledge

You can receive a free copy of your credit report every 12 months or when you are declined for credit.

- ❑ True
- ❑ False

☐ True Correct Answer

Sections of Credit Report

I. Identifying Information

II. Public Record Information

III. Credit History

IV. Inquires

Sections of Credit Report

I. Identifying Information

Includes your personal information such as your name, current and previous addresses, social security number, date of birth, etc.

II. Public Record Information

Contains information from local, state, and federal courts.

Sections of Credit Report

III. Credit History

Includes accounts creditors have turned over to any collection agency. Also, open and closed accounts are listed under this section.

Note: The credit history on a credit report is broken down in categories.

Sections of Credit Report

III. Credit History Categories

- Category 1 is where you will find the creditor who reported the information to your credit report. The creditor can be a department store, bank, hospital, auto finance company, credit card company, loan company, etc.
- Category 2 list the account number reported by the creditor. It may list only a few digits of the account number to protect your privacy.
- Category 3 shows the responsible party of the reported credit account.

  (*"J" = Joint you and another person, "I"= Individual only yourself.*)
- Category 4 shows the date (*only month and year*) the credit account was opened.

Sections of Credit Report

III. Credit History Categories….cont'd

- Category 5 shows the date of the last payment or the date of the last activity on the account.
- Category 6 lists the type of credit account. (*"R"= Revolving example credit card, "I" = Installment example car loan.*)
- Category 7 shows the payment status of the account. (*This may include the type of account along with the payment status. For example R1 = revolving account that was paid on-time or paid as agreed.*)
- Category 8 shows the credit limit for revolving accounts or the maximum loan amount owed for installment accounts.

Sections of Credit Report

III. Credit History Categories....cont'd

- Category 9 shows the monthly payment amount for the credit account.
- Category 10 is the remaining balance owed as of the date reported.
- Category 11 shows past due amount, if any.
- Category 12 shows the date the credit account was reported.
- Category 13 indicates the number of times the credit account has been 30, 60, or 90+ days past due.
- Category 14 miscellaneous.....type of account (*auto loan, credit card, mortgage loan, etc.*), the status of the account (*closed, paid, or charged off, etc.*).

Sections of Credit Report

IV. Inquires

Inquiries are listing of the name of a credit grantor (*one who grants you credit*), who has accessed your credit report. Each inquiry is posted to the credit file so you will know who has pulled your credit report. "Promotional" inquires aka soft inquires (for *example; pre-approved credit card application*) do not impact your credit score.

Credit

Things to Remember

- Request a copy of your Consumer Credit Report once every 12 months from all three nationwide credit reporting agencies: EQUIFAX, EXPERIAN, & TRANSUNION.

- Once you receive your credit report use the credit report itemization worksheet to transfer information from your report to the worksheet to simplify and view at-a-glance.

- On the following sheet, credit report – aged accounts, configure the length of time an account has been on your report from the time the account was opened to the current date. (Use the Time Calculator Link to configure timeframe: https://www.timeanddate.com/date/timeduration.html)

For more information on obtaining your free credit report visit www.annualcreditreport.com or call 1-877-322-8228. Deaf and hard of hearing consumers can access the TDD service by calling 7-1-1 and referring the Relay Operator to 1-800-821-7232.

Extra sheets have been provided.

Credit Report Itemization

NAME OF CREDITOR	OUTSTANDING BALANCE	AMOUNT PAST DUE	CREDITOR PHONE#	CREDITOR ADDRESS	STATUS OF ACCOUNT
MEDICAL					
Total	$	$			
COLLECTIONS					
Total	$	$			

Credit Report Itemization
continued…

NAME OF CREDITOR	OUTSTANDING BALANCE	AMOUNT PAST DUE	CREDITOR PHONE#	CREDITOR ADDRESS	STATUS OF ACCOUNT
ACCOUNTS					
Total	$	$			
OTHER					
Total	$	$			
GRAND TOTAL	$	$			

For more resources, please visit https://www.ofpsagency.com

Credit Report -Aged Accounts

ACCOUNT NUMBER	NAME OF CREDITOR	TYPE OF DEBT	AGED-ACCOUNT (Account Opened Date)	CONFIGURE TIMEFRAME (OPEN DATE from CURRENT DATE)	OPENED/CLOSED

Keep in mind, closing your oldest account could significantly reduce your credit score.

Credit Report Itemization

NAME OF CREDITOR	OUTSTANDING BALANCE	AMOUNT PAST DUE	CREDITOR PHONE#	CREDITOR ADDRESS	STATUS OF ACCOUNT
MEDICAL					
Total	$	$			
COLLECTIONS					
Total	$	$			

For more resources, please visit https://www.ofpsagency.com

Credit Report Itemization
continued...

NAME OF CREDITOR	OUTSTANDING BALANCE	AMOUNT PAST DUE	CREDITOR PHONE#	CREDITOR ADDRESS	STATUS OF ACCOUNT
ACCOUNTS					
Total	$	$			
OTHER					
Total	$	$			
GRAND TOTAL	$	$			

For more resources, please visit https://www.ofpsagency.com

Credit Report -Aged Accounts

ACCOUNT NUMBER	NAME OF CREDITOR	TYPE OF DEBT	AGED-ACCOUNT (Account Opened Date)	CONFIGURE TIMEFRAME (OPEN DATE from CURRENT DATE)	OPENED/CLOSED

Keep in mind, closing your oldest account could significantly reduce your credit score.

For more resources, please visit https://www.ofpsagency.com

Credit Report Itemization

NAME OF CREDITOR	OUTSTANDING BALANCE	AMOUNT PAST DUE	CREDITOR PHONE#	CREDITOR ADDRESS	STATUS OF ACCOUNT
MEDICAL					
Total	$	$			
COLLECTIONS					
Total	$	$			

Credit Report Itemization

continued…

NAME OF CREDITOR	OUTSTANDING BALANCE	AMOUNT PAST DUE	CREDITOR PHONE#	CREDITOR ADDRESS	STATUS OF ACCOUNT
ACCOUNTS					
Total	$	$			
OTHER					
Total	$	$			
GRAND TOTAL	$	$			

For more resources, please visit https://www.ofpsagency.com

Credit Report -Aged Accounts

ACCOUNT NUMBER	NAME OF CREDITOR	TYPE OF DEBT	AGED-ACCOUNT (Account Opened Date)	CONFIGURE TIMEFRAME (OPEN DATE from CURRENT DATE)	OPENED/CLOSED

Keep in mind, closing your oldest account could significantly reduce your credit score.

Test Your Knowledge

If you are a credit card holder, how much of the credit limit should be used to retain a good credit score?

Select the <u>BEST</u> answer.

- ❑ The entire credit limit.
- ❑ Never spend no more than 50% of your credit card limit.
- ❑ Spend no more than 20%-30% of the total credit limit on any credit card.

❑ Spend no more than 20%-30% of the total credit limit on any credit card. Correct Answer

Take Action

ACCOUNT LOG SHEET

"Unlock the door of your mind with the key of KNOWLEDGE."–Stacey M. Oliver

Account Log

	WEBSITE LINK	ACCOUNT#	*USERNAME*	*PASSWORD*
LOANS				
EXAMPLE: World Finance	https://www.loansbyworld.com/	987456321	JonDoe1	3JoN!Do3
CREDIT CARDS/LINE OF CREDIT				
UTILITIES				
AUTO INSURANCE				

Account Log

	WEBSITE LINK	ACCOUNT#	*USERNAME*	*PASSWORD*
LOANS				
CREDIT CARDS/LINE OF CREDIT				
UTILITIES				
AUTO INSURANCE				

Account Log *continued...*

	WEBSITE LINK	ACCOUNT#	*USERNAME*	*PASSWORD*
PERSONAL BANK ACCOUNTS				
BUSINESS BANK ACCOUNTS				
INVESTMENTS AND RETIREMENT				
LIFE INSURANCE				

Quick Reminders

GLOSSARY
&
RESOURCES

Glossary

- **Credit**: no upfront payment for purchases based on the trust that payment will be made in the future: refer to one's spending/payment reputation status: the provision of money, goods, or services with the expectation of future payment.
- **Creditworthy**: financially sound and stabled to justify the extension of credit.
- **Credit Card**: open-end loans with a certain limit used by individuals to pay for everyday expenses/purchases or provide cash advances to be paid over a period of time which may incur interest on any outstanding loan balance.
- **Credit Report**: an individual's record of having borrowed and repaid money: payment history on recent and past obligations.
- **Credit Score**: numbers created by mathematical formulas that use individuals' credit history to calculate their score.
- **Debt – to – Income (DTI) Ratio**: measures the amount of income a person generates in order to pay debt responsibly.
- **Installment Loan**: typically for big ticket items such as home, vehicles, etc.
- **Minimum payment**: lowest dollar amount required to be paid each month on a loan, credit card, or other debt.

Glossary

- **Revolving Credit**: commonly used for everyday purchases like food, gas, clothes, etc.: Accounts that do not require to pay outstanding balances in full.
- **Secured Loan**: loans in which property owned by individuals are used as collateral.
- **Unsecured Loan**: no property is used for collateral (most common type is credit cards).

Resources

Equifax	Experian	TransUnion
P.O. Box 74241	701 Experian Parkway	Two Baldwin Place
1150 Lake Hearn Drive	P. O. Box 2002	P.O. Box 1000
Suite 460	Allen, TX 75013-0036	Chester, PA 19022
Atlanta, GA 30374	1-888-397-3742	1-800-888-4213
1-800-685-1111		

Resources continued...

Annual Credit Report Link: https://www.annualcreditreport.com/index.action

Credit Cards: https://www.creditcards.com/rewards-cards/

Equifax Link: www.equifax.com

Experian Link: www.experian.com

FICO Score Link: https://creditscorecard.com/

Identity Theft: https://www.identitytheft.gov/Assistant

Opt-Out Online Link: https://www.donotcall.gov/default.aspx

Reward Cards for Points (Compare Cards by Lending Tree): https://www.comparecards.com/reward?utm

Time Calculator Link: https://www.timeanddate.com/date/timeduration.html

TransUnion Link: www.transunion.com

Calendar

MONTH ______________________________ **YEAR** ________________

Sunday	Monday	Tuesday	Wednesday	Thursday	Friday	Saturday

Calendar

MONTH ______________________________ **YEAR** ________________

Sunday	Monday	Tuesday	Wednesday	Thursday	Friday	Saturday

For more resources, please visit https://www.ofpsagency.com

Calendar

MONTH ______________________ **YEAR** ______________

Sunday	Monday	Tuesday	Wednesday	Thursday	Friday	Saturday

Calendar

MONTH ______________________				YEAR ____________		
Sunday	Monday	Tuesday	Wednesday	Thursday	Friday	Saturday

Calendar

MONTH ________________________________ **YEAR** ________________

Sunday	Monday	Tuesday	Wednesday	Thursday	Friday	Saturday

Calendar

MONTH ______________________________ YEAR ________________

Sunday	Monday	Tuesday	Wednesday	Thursday	Friday	Saturday

Memo Notes

Memo Notes

Memo Notes

Memo Notes

Memo Notes

Stay Connected

Olivers Financial Planning Services, LLC
(aka OFPS, LLC)

www.ofpsagency.com

https://instagram.com/oliversfps

http://www.twitter.com/Ofpsllc

http://www.facebook.com/Oliversfps

Olivers Financial Planning Services, LLC ®TM

PO Box 51363
Piedmont, SC 29673
Email: ofpsagency@outlook.com

Made in the USA
Las Vegas, NV
03 November 2026

57425292R00045